Artificial Intelligence in Accounting: Manual for Expert Accountants

Future Perspectives and Tips for Adapting
to Artificial Intelligence in Accounting   31

**Appendix: Useful Resources for Further
Study**   32

Brief Description of Online Tools and
Resources for Artificial Intelligence in
Accounting   34

Artificial Intelligence in Accounting:
Manual for Expert Accountants

The digital revolution has brought with it the advent of Artificial Intelligence in the accounting field, offering expert accountants new opportunities and challenges to face. This manual is designed specifically for those who deal with administration and accounting management with the use of Artificial Intelligence, providing detailed guidance on how to integrate this cutting-edge technology into their daily work.

In these pages, we will explore the different applications of Artificial Intelligence in accounting, from automatic invoice recognition to cash flow forecasting, through predictive analysis of financial data. Experienced accountants will learn to make the most of the technological tools available to optimize accounting processes, reducing human errors and increasing the overall efficiency of their work.

Through practical examples and case studies, the best practices for integrating Artificial Intelligence into accounting management will be illustrated, ensuring maximum precision and reliability in the results obtained. Readers will discover how to best use specialized accounting software based on Artificial Intelligence and how to adapt their professional skills to this new, constantly evolving technological scenario.

With this manual, expert accountants will be able to expand their knowledge and skills, keeping up with the latest innovations in the accounting sector and fully exploiting the potential of Artificial Intelligence to offer an even more effective and high-quality service to their clients.

Chapter 1: Introduction to Artificial Intelligence in Accounting

What is Artificial Intelligence

What is Artificial Intelligence

Artificial Intelligence (AI) represents one of the most revolutionary technologies of our time in the accounting field. For experienced accountants engaged in accounting administration and management with Artificial Intelligence, fully understanding what AI is is essential to exploit its full potential.

In simple terms, Artificial Intelligence refers to the ability of machines to imitate human intelligence. This means that AI systems can learn, reason and make decisions autonomously, without being explicitly programmed to perform certain tasks. Thanks to the use of complex algorithms and machine learning, AI allows you to analyze huge amounts of data quickly, identifying patterns and providing precise predictions.

Artificial Intelligence in Accounting: Manual for Expert Accountants

In the context of accounting, AI can revolutionize the way accounting processes are managed, making them more efficient, accurate and automated. Experienced accountants who embrace this technology will be able to focus on more strategic and value-enhancing activities, leaving repetitive and tedious tasks to machines.

In this manual dedicated to Artificial Intelligence in accounting, we will explore the different practical applications of AI for accountants, providing suggestions and best practices for successfully integrating this technology into their daily activities. Let's prepare to seize the challenges and opportunities offered by AI in accounting and drive change towards a more innovative and efficient future.

Applications of Artificial Intelligence in Accounting

The applications of Artificial Intelligence in accounting represent an unprecedented revolution in the accounting administration and management sector. Thanks to the advent of cutting-edge technologies, accountants have tools capable of automating complex processes, optimizing resources and improving operational efficiency.

Systems based on Artificial Intelligence allow you to analyze large quantities of data in real time, identify patterns and trends, as well as predict future scenarios with high precision. This translates into greater decision-making capacity on the part of accountants, who can process detailed and strategic information to best support their clients.

Artificial Intelligence in Accounting: Manual for Expert Accountants

Summary

Artificial Intelligence in Accounting: Manual for Expert Accountants	4
Chapter 1: Introduction to Artificial Intelligence in Accounting	5
What is Artificial Intelligence	5
Applications of Artificial Intelligence in Accounting	6
Benefits of Using Artificial Intelligence for Accountants	7
Chapter 2: Accounting Fundamentals and Automation	9
Basic Accounting Concepts	9
Automation of Accounting Processes	10
Impact of Artificial Intelligence on Accounting Management	11
Chapter 3: Tools and Technologies for Artificial Intelligence in Accounting	13
Accounting Software based on Artificial Intelligence	13
Machine Learning and Accounting	14
Predictive Analysis and Financial Reporting	15

Artificial Intelligence in Accounting: Manual for Expert Accountants

Chapter 4: Practical Implementation of Artificial Intelligence in Accounting   16

    Integration of Accounting Systems with Artificial Intelligence   16

    Risks and Challenges in the Adoption of Artificial Intelligence   18

    Best Practices for Using Artificial Intelligence in Accounting   19

Chapter 5: Ethics and Safety in the Use of Artificial Intelligence   20

    Ethical Implications of Artificial Intelligence in Accounting   20

    Data Protection and Customer Privacy   22

    Role of Accountants in Guaranteeing Transparency and Security   23

Chapter 6: Future of Artificial Intelligence in Accounting   24

    Emerging Trends in Artificial Intelligence and Accounting   24

    Possible Developments and Innovations in the Accounting Sector   25

    Role of Accountants in the Age of Artificial Intelligence   27

Conclusions   28

Impact of Artificial Intelligence on the Profession of Accountants   30

Artificial Intelligence in Accounting: Manual for Expert Accountants

The main applications of Artificial Intelligence in accounting include the automatic categorization of transactions, the detection of fraud and anomalies, the generation of personalized reports and the optimization of budgeting and forecasting processes. Furthermore, Artificial Intelligence systems are able to interact with customers in a more intuitive and personalized way, improving the overall collaboration experience.

For accountants expert in the use of Artificial Intelligence, the opportunity to offer innovative and high added value services presents itself as a fundamental competitive advantage. Through the knowledge and implementation of these cutting-edge technologies, accounting professionals can radically transform their working approach, providing increasingly efficient and targeted solutions to the specific needs of clients.

In conclusion, Artificial Intelligence represents a fundamental resource for accountants engaged in accounting administration and management, opening up new prospects for growth and professional development in the increasingly digital and advanced context of the sector.

Benefits of Using Artificial Intelligence for Accountants

The benefits of using Artificial Intelligence for Accountants

Artificial Intelligence in Accounting: Manual for Expert Accountants

Artificial Intelligence (AI) is revolutionizing the accounting industry, offering accountants innovative tools to optimize their daily activities. The benefits deriving from the use of AI are multiple and have a positive impact on the efficiency and precision of the work carried out by professionals in the sector.

One of the main benefits of AI for accountants is the ability to automate repetitive and tedious processes, allowing them to focus on high-value-added activities. Thanks to AI, accountants can reduce data processing times, eliminate human errors and improve the overall quality of services offered to their clients.

Furthermore, AI allows accountants to analyze large amounts of data quickly, providing them with in-depth insights into the financial situation of the companies they follow. This predictive ability of AI allows accountants to provide proactive advice to their clients, supporting them in financial planning and strategic management of their business.

Thanks to AI, accountants can also improve the security of their clients' sensitive data by implementing advanced encryption and information protection solutions. This not only guarantees compliance with current regulations regarding privacy, but also increases customer confidence in the professionalism and reliability of the accountant.

In conclusion, the use of Artificial Intelligence represents a great opportunity for expert accountants in the field of accounting administration and management, allowing them to offer high quality, efficient and personalized services to their clients, thus maintaining a competitive advantage in the constantly evolving market.

Chapter 2: Fundamentals of Accounting and Automation

Basic Accounting Concepts

Basic Accounting Concepts

Accounting is the financial language of business, a system of monitoring and recording transactions that occur within an organization. For accountants experienced in the field of Accounting Administration and Management with Artificial Intelligence, understanding the basic concepts of accounting is essential to be able to correctly interpret financial data and make informed decisions.

The main basic concepts of accounting include the principle of double recording, according to which every financial transaction must be recorded twice, once as a credit and once as a debit. This ensures that the budget is always in balance.

Another key concept is the difference between assets, liabilities and equity. Assets represent what the company owns, liabilities are what the company owes, and net worth is the difference between assets and liabilities, which represents the value of the owners' investments.

Furthermore, it is important to understand the concept of the accrual principle, according to which revenues and expenses must be recorded in the period in which they are generated, regardless of when the money is actually received or paid.

These are just some of the basic accounting concepts that accountants experienced in using Artificial Intelligence must master to fully exploit the potential of technology in accounting management.

Automation of Accounting Processes

In the world of accounting, the introduction of Artificial Intelligence has revolutionized accounting processes, bringing tangible benefits for expert accountants and for companies that manage accounting administration with the help of innovative technologies. The automation of accounting processes represents a fundamental step towards efficiency and accuracy in the sector.

Artificial Intelligence in Accounting: Manual for Expert Accountants

Automation helps minimize human errors, improving the quality of accounting operations and allowing accountants to focus on high-value-added activities. Thanks to Artificial Intelligence, repetitive tasks such as data entry, transaction classification and report generation can be automated, allowing professionals to save precious time and focus on more strategic tasks.

One of the main benefits of automating accounting processes is the speed with which information is processed and analyzed, allowing for greater timeliness in business decisions. Furthermore, the use of Artificial Intelligence allows us to identify hidden patterns and trends in accounting data, providing accountants with valuable insights to optimize the financial performance of companies.

In this context, it is essential that expert accountants acquire skills in the use of intelligent technologies to guarantee a cutting-edge service in line with market needs. The automation of accounting processes is not only an opportunity to improve operational efficiency, but also to offer a more qualified and value-oriented consultancy service for customers.

Impact of Artificial Intelligence on Accounting Management
" Impact of Artificial Intelligence on Accounting Management

Artificial Intelligence in Accounting: Manual for Expert Accountants

The advent of Artificial Intelligence (AI) has profoundly revolutionized the accounting management sector, offering new opportunities and exciting challenges for experienced accountants. This sub-chapter aims to take a closer look at how AI is influencing accounting practice and how industry professionals can best capitalize on this change.

With the introduction of advanced AI systems, accounting processes have become more efficient and effective. Thanks to AI's ability to analyze large amounts of data in real time, accountants can gain insights and accurate predictions to support business decisions. Furthermore, repetitive and tedious tasks can be automated, allowing professionals to focus on high-value added activities.

However, adopting AI in accounting management also presents unique challenges. It is crucial that accountants acquire technical skills to best use AI-based tools and understand the ethical implications of automating decision-making processes.

In conclusion, Artificial Intelligence is redefining the accounting management landscape, offering unprecedented opportunities to optimize operations and improve the quality of services offered by expert accountants. It is essential for industry professionals to embrace this transformation and develop the skills needed to successfully lead businesses into the digital future.

Chapter 3: Tools and Technologies for Artificial Intelligence in Accounting

Accounting Software based on Artificial Intelligence

Accounting Software based on Artificial Intelligence

The use of cutting-edge technologies such as Artificial Intelligence is revolutionizing the accounting sector, offering new opportunities for expert accountants working in the field of accounting administration and management. Accounting software based on Artificial Intelligence represents an indispensable resource for optimizing processes, reducing errors and increasing the efficiency of daily work.

Thanks to the ability of machine learning and predictive analysis, these software are able to process huge amounts of data quickly, providing accurate and detailed results. Accountants who embrace this innovation can benefit from greater accuracy in calculations, better cash flow management and deeper insight into business performance.

Furthermore, Accounting Software based on Artificial Intelligence allows you to automate repetitive tasks and manual work, freeing up precious time that can be dedicated to consultancy and strategic analysis activities for clients. This digital transformation not only improves operational efficiency, but also helps to enhance the role of the accountant as a trusted advisor and strategic partner for businesses.

Artificial Intelligence in Accounting: Manual for Expert Accountants

To remain competitive in the modern accounting landscape, expert accountants must embrace the potential offered by Artificial Intelligence-based Accounting Software and integrate them into their professional practice, making the most of the opportunities for growth and innovation that they represent.

Machine Learning and Accounting

Machine Learning and Accounting

Machine Learning represents one of the most revolutionary technologies in accounting and business administration. Thanks to its ability to analyze huge amounts of data quickly and efficiently, Machine Learning allows accountants to obtain detailed and predictive information to support financial and management decisions.

In the context of accounting administration and management, Artificial Intelligence (AI) and Machine Learning can be used to automate repetitive and redundant processes, improving efficiency and reducing human errors. For example, machine learning models can be used for accounting data analysis, fraud detection, cash flow forecasting, and financial risk management.

Artificial Intelligence in Accounting: Manual for Expert Accountants

Experienced accountants who want to stay ahead of the curve and offer high-quality service to their clients should familiarize themselves with Machine Learning concepts and understand how to integrate them into their accounting practice. This manual provides guidelines and best practices for implementing Artificial Intelligence in accounting, helping professionals to fully exploit the potential of these innovative technologies.

In an era where digitalization and automation are transforming the way financial data is managed, Machine Learning presents itself as a fundamental tool for optimizing accounting processes and improving the accuracy and effectiveness of financial analyses. Accountants who are able to capitalize on the potential of Machine Learning will have a significant competitive advantage in the accounting and business administration sector.

Predictive Analysis and Financial Reporting

Predictive Analysis and Financial Reporting

Predictive analytics and financial reporting are two fundamental pillars in the application of artificial intelligence in the accounting field. Experienced accountants working in AI-powered accounting management must master these skills to stay ahead of the challenges and opportunities of the modern financial world.

Predictive analytics uses advanced algorithms to analyze past and present financial data to identify trends, patterns and predictions for the future. Thanks to artificial intelligence, accountants can obtain more accurate and timely forecasts, supporting business decisions with information based on solid and reliable data.

Financial reporting, on the other hand, involves the creation of detailed, customized reports that highlight the company's financial situation clearly and accurately. With the help of artificial intelligence, accountants can automate the report generation process, reducing errors and work time and ensuring greater precision and consistency in the analysis of financial data.

In this constantly evolving context, expert accountants must be able to correctly interpret the results of predictive analysis and financial reporting, translating them into concrete strategies and actions to improve company performance. Artificial intelligence is a precious ally that, if used effectively, can radically transform the way accounting is conducted, leading to more efficient, precise and business success-oriented results.

Chapter 4: Practical Implementation of Artificial Intelligence in Accounting

Integration of Accounting Systems with Artificial Intelligence

Integration of Accounting Systems with Artificial Intelligence

Artificial Intelligence in Accounting: Manual for Expert Accountants

The integration of accounting systems with artificial intelligence represents a fundamental turning point in the field of accounting administration and management. Thanks to the potential offered by AI, expert accountants can significantly improve the efficiency and accuracy of accounting processes.

The adoption of artificial intelligence allows accounting professionals to automate a number of repetitive and tedious tasks, allowing them to focus on high-value-added activities. AI-based systems can analyze large amounts of data in real time, spotting patterns and anomalies that would otherwise have escaped the human eye.

Furthermore, artificial intelligence is able to provide forecasts and suggestions based on predictive models, supporting accountants in developing more robust and targeted financial strategies. Thanks to these features, professionals can offer a more personalized service oriented towards the specific needs of their clients.

It is vital that accountants familiarize themselves with AI-based technologies and fully understand their potential. Only through constant training and an openness towards innovation will it be possible to fully exploit the advantages offered by this digital revolution in the accounting field.

In conclusion, the integration of accounting systems with artificial intelligence represents a unique opportunity for expert accountants to stand out on the market, offering cutting-edge and high-quality services in the field of accounting administration and management.

Risks and Challenges in the Adoption of Artificial Intelligence

Risks and Challenges in Adopting Artificial Intelligence

The introduction of artificial intelligence in the field of accounting administration and management represents a revolutionary turning point for expert accountants. However, with technological innovation, risks and challenges also arise that need to be addressed with care and preparation.

One of the main risks in adopting artificial intelligence is related to the privacy and security of sensitive customer data. With increasingly complex algorithms and machine learning capabilities, it is essential to ensure data protection and comply with privacy regulations such as GDPR.

Furthermore, over-reliance on AI could lead to a loss of control by expert accountants. It is crucial to maintain a balance between accounting process automation and human involvement to ensure accuracy and correct interpretation of data.

Artificial Intelligence in Accounting: Manual for Expert Accountants

The challenges do not only concern the technological aspect, but also the training and adaptation of professionals. Experienced accountants must be prepared to learn new skills and fully understand how AI works to reap its full benefits.

In conclusion, the adoption of artificial intelligence in accounting administration and management offers numerous opportunities, but it is essential to be aware of the risks and challenges it entails. Only through adequate preparation and a holistic vision of technological innovation will it be possible to maximize the advantages of this revolution in the accounting field.

Best Practices for Using Artificial Intelligence in Accounting

Accountants who are experts in accounting administration and management with artificial intelligence are called upon to implement best practices to fully exploit the potential of these technologies. In this chapter we will explore the most effective strategies for using artificial intelligence in accounting, optimizing processes and improving the quality of the work performed.

One of the best practices is to automate repetitive and tedious tasks through the use of advanced accounting software. Artificial intelligence can be used to automatically classify transactions, generate detailed reports and identify anomalies in financial data, allowing accountants to focus on higher value-added activities.

Another key practice is to implement machine learning systems to predict financial trends, identify potential risks and investment opportunities, and improve cash flow forecasting. Predictive analysis carried out by artificial intelligence can provide accountants with crucial information to support business decisions and optimize financial management.

Finally, it is essential to constantly train staff on new developments in artificial intelligence and digital accounting, ensuring correct implementation of the technologies and maximizing the benefits for the professional firm and clients.

By implementing these best practices, accountants will be able to fully reap the benefits of artificial intelligence in accounting, improving operational efficiency, data accuracy and the quality of the service offered.

Chapter 5: Ethics and Safety in the Use of Artificial Intelligence

Ethical Implications of Artificial Intelligence in Accounting

Artificial Intelligence in Accounting: Manual for Expert Accountants

The ethical implications of artificial intelligence in accounting represent a topic of crucial importance for expert accountants specializing in accounting administration and management with artificial intelligence. The advent and diffusion of increasingly advanced technologies in the field of accounting pose ethical challenges that require careful reflection and regulation.

Using algorithms and artificial intelligence systems to automate accounting processes can lead to greater efficiency and precision in calculations, reducing the margin of human error. However, it is crucial to consider the ethical implications related to transparency, accountability and data security. Accountants must ensure that the systems used are reliable, respect data privacy and comply with current regulations.

Furthermore, the use of artificial intelligence raises questions about the impact on traditional jobs and the role of accounting professionals. It is necessary to carefully address the dynamics of change in the labor market and ensure a fair transition for all actors involved.

Dialogue between accountants, AI experts and legislators is essential to develop appropriate ethical and regulatory guidelines to regulate the use of AI in accounting. Only through synergistic and proactive collaboration will it be possible to maximize the benefits of these technologies, while minimizing risks and preserving the fundamental ethical values of the accounting profession.

Data Protection and Customer Privacy

Data protection and customer privacy are issues of fundamental importance in the field of Accounting Administration and Management with Artificial Intelligence. Experienced accountants must be particularly careful to ensure the security of sensitive information processed in information systems, especially considering the growing diffusion of intelligent technologies.

To protect customer data, it is essential to take appropriate security measures, such as using encryption to protect communications and stored data, managing access permissions on a need-to-know basis, and continuously monitoring for identify and prevent any violations.

Furthermore, it is essential to comply with privacy regulations, such as the GDPR, which establishes clear rules on the processing of personal data. Accountants must inform their clients about the purpose and method of using the data, obtaining explicit consent when necessary.

Adopting best practices in data protection and client privacy not only ensures legal compliance, but also helps maintain client trust and protect the firm's reputation. In an era where data management is increasingly crucial, accountants must be ready to face cybersecurity challenges with competence and responsibility.

Role of Accountants in Guaranteeing Transparency and Security

The role of accountants in guaranteeing transparency and security represents a fundamental pillar in the field of accounting administration and management with artificial intelligence. Experienced accountants are called upon to perform an important supervisory and control function, ensuring that accounting processes comply with current regulations and that financial data is accurate and truthful.

The advent of artificial intelligence has revolutionized the accounting sector, introducing tools and technologies capable of automating numerous tasks and optimizing processes. However, the human presence of accountants remains indispensable to ensure the correct implementation and functioning of these systems, as well as to correctly interpret the data generated in order to provide strategic advice to clients.

Transparency and security of accounting data are crucial elements to ensure the trust of investors, financial institutions and regulators. Accountants, with their competence and professionalism, are able to guarantee the correct management and protection of financial information, reducing the risk of fraud and errors to a minimum.

In an increasingly digitalized and complex environment, experienced accountants play a key role in promoting the responsible adoption of artificial intelligence in the accounting sector, ensuring that the benefits arising from this technology are accompanied by strict compliance with regulations and ethical standards .

Chapter 6: Future of Artificial Intelligence in Accounting

Emerging Trends in Artificial Intelligence and Accounting

Emerging trends in Artificial Intelligence are revolutionizing the accounting industry, offering new opportunities and challenges for experienced accountants in the field of accounting administration and management with Artificial Intelligence.

Artificial Intelligence in Accounting: Manual for Expert Accountants

In this chapter we will explore how AI is transforming the way accounting processes are managed, improving efficiency and reducing human errors. Thanks to the automation of repetitive tasks and the ability to analyze large amounts of data quickly, accountants can focus on high-value activities, such as financial analysis and strategic consultancy.

Emerging technologies such as machine learning and deep learning are allowing AI solutions to learn from data and continuously improve their performance, making it possible to identify patterns and anomalies more precisely and efficiently.

Furthermore, the use of chatbots and virtual assistants is simplifying communication with customers and improving the overall accounting experience, allowing for greater interaction and faster resolution of requests.

It is crucial for accountants to stay up-to-date on the latest trends and developments in AI to take full advantage of the opportunities presented by this constantly evolving technology and provide a high-quality service to their clients.

Possible Developments and Innovations in the Accounting Sector

Artificial Intelligence in Accounting: Manual for Expert Accountants

In the ever-evolving world of accounting, artificial intelligence is quickly establishing itself as a game-changing innovation in the industry. Experienced accountants are faced with new challenges and opportunities, as the integration of AI into accounting management brings with it a number of possible developments and innovations.

One of the main benefits of using AI in accounting is the ability to automate repetitive and redundant processes, allowing accountants to focus on high-value-added activities. Thanks to AI, it is possible to improve operational efficiency, reduce human errors and provide more accurate predictive analytics.

Furthermore, AI opens the door to new consultancy opportunities for accountants, allowing them to offer more detailed and in-depth, personalized, data-driven services. AI's ability to analyze large volumes of data in real time allows accountants to provide their clients with a more accurate and in-depth view of their finances.

However, it is important for accountants to be aware of the possible risks of using AI in accounting, such as data security and privacy. It is crucial to take appropriate security measures and ensure regulatory compliance to avoid potential problems.

In conclusion, possible developments and innovations in AI accounting offer experienced accountants the opportunity to improve efficiency, provide more advanced consultancy services and maintain a competitive advantage in the ever-evolving accounting management market. .

Role of Accountants in the Age of Artificial Intelligence

Role of Accountants in the Age of Artificial Intelligence

The advent of Artificial Intelligence has revolutionized the accounting administration and management sector, posing new challenges but also great opportunities for expert accountants. The role of these professionals evolves in a context in which digital technology plays an increasingly relevant role.

The introduction of tools based on Artificial Intelligence allows accountants to optimize accounting processes, automating repetitive tasks and allowing greater precision and timeliness in data processing. However, this does not mean that the human role becomes superfluous. On the contrary, accountants are called upon to play a role in supervising and interpreting the data generated by new technologies.

Artificial Intelligence in Accounting: Manual for Expert Accountants

In an environment where regulatory complexity is constantly evolving, experienced accountants are essential to ensuring compliance with tax and accounting regulations, as well as providing strategic advice to client companies. The ability to understand and effectively use tools based on Artificial Intelligence therefore becomes a distinctive element for professionals in the sector.

To remain competitive in the era of Artificial Intelligence, accountants must invest in their training and professional development, acquiring digital skills and data analysis skills. Only in this way will they be able to fully exploit the potential offered by technology to improve the quality of the services offered and consolidate their position on the market.

In conclusion, the role of accountants in the era of Artificial Intelligence is evolving towards greater integration between human and technological skills, offering new opportunities for growth and professional development in the accounting administration and management sector.

Conclusions
Conclusions

Artificial Intelligence in Accounting: Manual for Expert Accountants

In this manual dedicated to the application of Artificial Intelligence in accounting, we have examined in detail how this technology is transforming the sector for experienced accountants. The adoption of Artificial Intelligence in accounting management offers numerous opportunities and challenges that require constant attention and updating from professionals in the sector.

One of the main conclusions that emerged is that Artificial Intelligence can significantly improve the efficiency and accuracy of accounting processes, allowing accountants to focus on high-value-added activities such as data analysis and strategic advice for clients. However, it is important to underline that AI will never completely replace the human role in accounting, but rather complement and enrich it.

To maximize the benefits of Artificial Intelligence, accountants must invest in training and developing digital skills, so they can fully exploit the potential of this technology. Furthermore, it is essential to maintain an ethical and responsible approach in the use of AI, ensuring the transparency and security of customer data.

In conclusion, Artificial Intelligence represents a great opportunity for expert accountants in the field of accounting management, but requires constant commitment to improving skills and adopting ethical practices. With the correct integration of AI into their daily work, accountants can offer an increasingly efficient and quality service to their clients, while maintaining a central role in the business decision-making process.

Impact of Artificial Intelligence on the Profession of Accountants

Impact of Artificial Intelligence on the Accounting Profession

Technological evolution in the field of accounting has brought an unprecedented transformation to the profession of accountants. The introduction of Artificial Intelligence (AI) has revolutionized accounting processes, offering new opportunities and challenges for those working in accounting administration and management.

AI has made it possible to automate many repetitive and tedious tasks, allowing accountants to focus on high-value-added tasks such as data analysis, strategic consulting and financial planning. Thanks to AI, accountants can process large amounts of data quickly, identify significant anomalies and trends, thus providing more timely and effective decision support to their clients.

However, the adoption of AI also entails a necessary transformation of the professional skills of accountants. It is essential to gain in-depth knowledge of emerging technologies, develop skills in data analytics and artificial intelligence, and adapt work processes to new industry dynamics.

In this context, it is essential that accountants maintain a proactive approach to innovation, investing in continuous training and professional development to remain competitive in an increasingly digitalized and globalized market. Only by embracing change and fully exploiting the potential of AI will accountants be able to offer a superior quality service to their clients and ensure the long-term success of their professional activity.

Future Perspectives and Tips for Adapting to Artificial Intelligence in Accounting

Future Perspectives and Tips for Adapting to Artificial Intelligence in Accounting

The advent of Artificial Intelligence (AI) in the field of accounting has led to notable changes and revolutions in the way we carry out our daily activities. For experienced accountants and those involved in accounting administration and management with Artificial Intelligence, it is essential to understand the future prospects and adapt to this new rapidly evolving reality.

The future prospects of using AI in accounting are broad and promising. AI is expected to continue to improve the efficiency and accuracy of accounting tasks, while reducing the risk of human error. Furthermore, AI could open up new opportunities to develop personalized services and high-level advice for customers.

To successfully adapt to AI in accounting, it is critical for accountants and management accountants to embrace change and invest in their education. It is advisable to acquire technical skills in using AI-based software and tools, as well as develop skills in data analysis and interpretation of information generated by AI.

Furthermore, it is important to maintain a proactive attitude in adopting new technologies and exploring the potential of AI to improve accounting processes and offer an increasingly efficient and personalized service to customers.

In conclusion, the future prospects of using Artificial Intelligence in accounting are exciting and full of opportunities for those who are willing to adapt and grow professionally in this ever-evolving field.

Appendix: Useful Resources for Further Study

Appendix: Useful Resources for Further Study

Artificial Intelligence in Accounting: Manual for Expert Accountants

In this section, we provide a list of valuable resources to delve deeper into the topic of Artificial Intelligence applied to accounting, aimed at expert accountants who operate in the field of accounting administration and management with the use of AI tools.

1. **Recommended Books**:
- "Artificial Intelligence for Accounting: Strategies and Practical Applications" by Luca Rossi.
- "Accounting 4.0: The Impact of AI on the World of Accounting" by Chiara Bianchi.

2. **Websites and Blogs**:
- AI4Accountants.it: A portal dedicated to the latest developments in Artificial Intelligence in the accounting sector.
- IlCommercialistaDigitale.com: Insights into the integration of AI into daily accounting practices.

3. **Events and Conferences**:
- National AI & Accounting Conference: An opportunity to meet industry experts and learn about the latest trends.
- "AI for Accountants" Webinar: Online sessions to understand how to make the most of AI in accounting management.

4. **Training Courses**:
- "Advanced Course on the Use of Artificial Intelligence in Accounting" at Bocconi University.
- "Master in Digital Accounting and Artificial Intelligence" offered by the Order of Accountants.

Deepening your knowledge of Artificial Intelligence in accounting is essential to remaining competitive in the market and offering cutting-edge services to your customers. Use these resources to broaden your skills and stay up to date on the latest technological innovations in the accounting industry.

Brief Description of Online Tools and Resources for Artificial Intelligence in Accounting

Brief Description of Online Tools and Resources for Artificial Intelligence in Accounting

In the increasingly digital landscape in which expert accountants operate in the field of administration and accounting management with artificial intelligence, it is essential to keep up with the latest technologies and online resources available.

Artificial intelligence tools dedicated to accounting are revolutionizing the way accounting processes are managed. Among the most useful and innovative online resources, automated accounting software stands out which uses advanced algorithms to analyze financial data, generate detailed reports and identify potential anomalies.

Furthermore, document management platforms based on artificial intelligence allow you to efficiently digitize and archive all accounting documents, facilitating the consultation and sharing of information in real time.

As for training resources, there are specialized online courses that offer insights into the application of artificial intelligence in accounting, providing accountants with the knowledge needed to fully exploit the potential of this technology.

In conclusion, the use of online tools and resources based on artificial intelligence represents a precious opportunity for expert accountants who wish to optimize accounting processes, improve efficiency and offer an increasingly innovative and cutting-edge service to their clients .

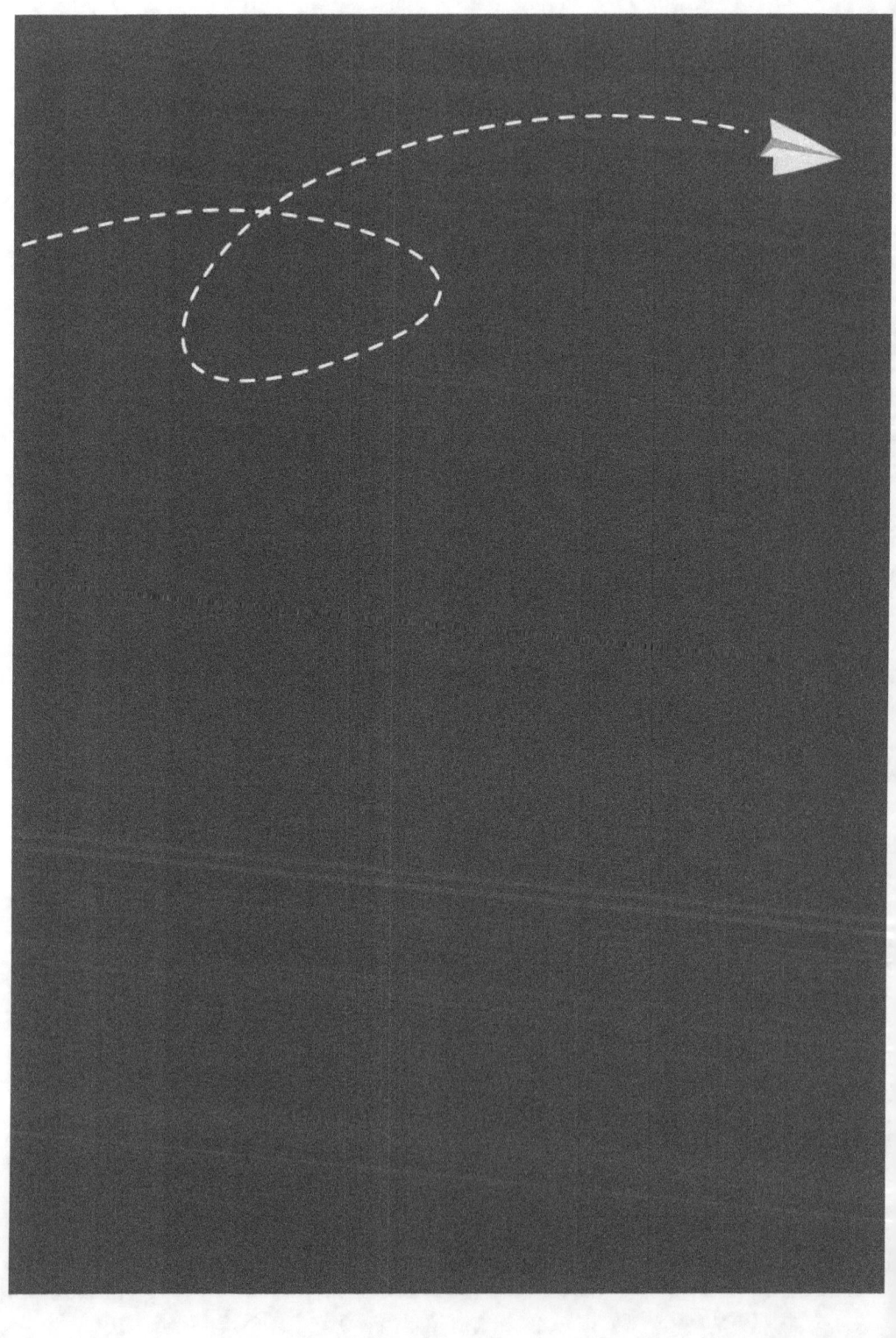

www.ingramcontent.com/pod-product-compliance
Lightning Source LLC
Chambersburg PA
CBHW070956220526
45471CB00007B/3056